Editor
Stephanie Buehler, Psy.D.

Contributing Editor
Wanda Kelly

Managing Editor
Ina Massler Levin, M.A.

Editor-in-Chief
Sharon Coan, M.S. Ed.

Cover Artist
Barb Lorseyedi

Art Coordinator
Kevin Barnes

Imaging
Alfred Lau
James Edward Grace

Product Manager
Phil Garcia

Publishers
Rachelle Cracchiolo, M.S. Ed.
Mary Dupuy Smith, M.S. Ed.

GRADE 3

Author

Wanda Kelly

Teacher Created Materials, Inc.
6421 Industry Way
Westminster, CA 92683
www.teachercreated.com

ISBN-0-7439-3342-7

©2002 Teacher Created Materials, Inc.
Reprinted, 2004
Made in U.S.A.

Table of Contents

Introduction

The old adage "practice makes perfect" can really hold true for your child and his or her education. The more practice and exposure your child has with concepts being taught in school, the more success he or she is likely to find. For many parents, knowing how to help their children may be frustrating because the resources may not be readily available.

Practice Makes Perfect: Writing Paragraphs, Grade 3, is a resource to help students practice and reinforce skills taught in the classroom. This book presents paragraph skills that are appropriate for third graders.

This book has six main sections, and each section is designed to meet one of the following objectives:

- Be familiar with the basic rules of grammar and spelling and identify and write complete sentences.
- Plan a paragraph before beginning to write.
- Develop a paragraph with a beginning, middle, and end.
- Revise and edit a paragraph by using specific details, varying sentence structure, and improving word choice.
- Proofread a paragraph by checking grammar, capitalization, punctuation, and spelling.
- Write paragraphs that explain, tell stories, relate personal experiences, and are letters to friends.

Throughout the book, students are asked to think critically and apply these skills. Students write various types of sentences and paragraphs, practice word usage and grammar, and work at revising their work. In the last section of the book, students can organize their own ideas and write original paragraphs and a friendly letter. In addition, there is a "Unit Assessment" on pages 46-47 that is presented in standardized test format so that students can practice their answers as they might see them in other settings.

The book includes an answer key for the practice exercises in the book and for the "Unit Assessment." Where students' answers will vary, examples are provided with the assignments.

How to Make the Most of This Book

Here are some useful ideas for making the most of this book:

- Set aside a specific place in your home to work on this book. Keep it neat and tidy, with the necessary materials on hand.
- Set up a certain time of day to work on these practice pages to establish consistency; or look for times in your day or week that are less hectic and conducive to practicing skills.
- Keep all practice sessions with your child positive and constructive. If your child becomes frustrated or tense, set the book aside and look for another time to practice. Forcing your child to perform will not help. Do not use this book as a punishment.
- Help beginning readers with instructions.
- Review the work your child has done.
- Pay attention to the areas in which your child has the most difficulty. Provide extra guidance and exercises in those areas.
- Look for ways to make real-life application to the skills being reinforced.

Sentences

There are four kinds of sentences: *declarative, interrogative, imperative,* and *exclamatory.*

- A *declarative* sentence makes a statement and ends with a period.

- An *interrogative* sentence asks a question and ends with a question mark.

- An *imperative* sentence makes a command and ends with a period.

- An *exclamatory* sentence shows strong emotion and ends with an exclamation point.

Label each sentence below with its type. Write **D** for declarative, **IT** for interrogative, **IP** for imperative, or **E** for exclamatory.

1. _____ Where did Jules go?

2. _____ He went to see Jessamine.

3. _____ What a lovely day!

4. _____ Sit up.

5. _____ Why did the bell ring early?

6. _____ Perhaps there was an emergency.

7. _____ Move that chair.

8. _____ I lost my wallet yesterday.

9. _____ It's hot!

10. _____ A magpie is black and white.

Write a question you would like to ask Abraham Lincoln.

_____

_____

Write a command you might give to a pet.

_____

_____

4

Capitalization

Always capitalize the following words:

- the first word in a sentence
- the pronoun *I*
- names of specific people and places
- titles when used with people's names or in place of their names

- days of the week and months
- key words in titles of publications, movies, songs, television shows, plays
- holidays

Rewrite each sentence to show correct capitalization.

1. when I went to the store I saw my teacher, mrs. lee.

_____

2. my family will go to disneyland in july.

_____

3. on wednesday we will celebrate groundhog day.

_____

4. in august we are going to visit aunt mary in san francisco, california.

_____

5. my neighbor julia is going to paris, france, next june.

_____

6. i am reading *old yeller* this week.

_____

7. my friend rosa speaks spanish, and i speak english.

_____

8. benjie had a birthday, and we sang "happy birthday to you."

_____

Punctuation

- Use appropriate ending punctuation (periods, question marks, and exclamation points).
- Use commas to separate words and phrases in a series, to separate a city and state (and after the state if the sentence continues), and to separate introductory words, phrases, and clauses from the rest of the sentence.
- Use apostrophes in contractions and with nouns and pronouns to indicate possession.
- Use quotation marks to show direct speech.

Rewrite the paragraph below, adding the correct punctuation.

On April Fools' Day

It was a clear calm day on April 1 2002 when I was a student at Oak Grove Elementary School in Oak Grove Montana My teacher came into the classroom and smiled Suddenly Jeffrey jumped up and said Mrs Lee theres a spider crawling on your head Oh said Glenda where is the spider Mrs Lee pretended that she was afraid but only for a minute Then Jeffrey yelled April Fool We all laughed Then Mrs Lee explained how the first day of April is always April Fools Day

_____

_____

_____

_____

_____

_____

_____

_____

_____

_____

Spelling

Rewrite the paragraph below, adding the correct spelling.

One day a boy woak up to get reddy for skool. He washt his fase and comed his hare. Then he put on the read shirt and blew genes that his mother had lade out for him. It took some time to put on his shews becawse the lases were tied in double nots. Finaly, he did it. Afterwards, he went to the kitchin to eat come serial and milk. It was verry good. Then he remembered he neaded to pak a lunch. He maid a peenut butter and jellee sandwitch, and he put it in his lunbox with an appel and some cookeys. Now he was reddy. But wait! He forgot to brush his teath. He brushed them quickly and finisht just as the buss was puling up. Then the boy was of to skool.

_____

_____

_____

_____

_____

_____

_____

_____

_____

_____

_____

_____

_____

_____

_____

_____

Assessment: The Basics

Respond to the following statements by writing the type of sentence listed for each one.

1. I wish that I could spend my vacation at the Grand Canyon.

   (interrogative sentence response) _____

   _____

2. You have just discovered that all your shoes are missing.

   (exclamatory sentence response) _____

   _____

3. You want your dog to stay in the backyard.

   (imperative sentence response) _____

   _____

4. Do you think the trees are prettier in the spring or in the fall?

   (declarative sentence response) _____

   _____

5. You have just learned that you have won a vacation trip to Hawaii.

   (interrogative sentence) _____

   _____

   (imperative sentence) _____

   _____

   (declarative sentence) _____

   _____

   (exclamatory sentence) _____

   _____

Assessment: The Basics (cont.)

Correct the capitalization, punctuation, and spelling when you rewrite the paragraph below.

a nite at the circuss

i love to go too the circuss on may 6 2002 the circuss kame to my homtown of jackson wyoming a parade marched threw are streats and soon the big top cud bee sean ken and i went to wach the performerrs prepare for openning nite we saw clowns acrobats and even the ringmaster what a site have you ever sean anything like it you shud go if you ever get the chance to spend a nite at the circuss

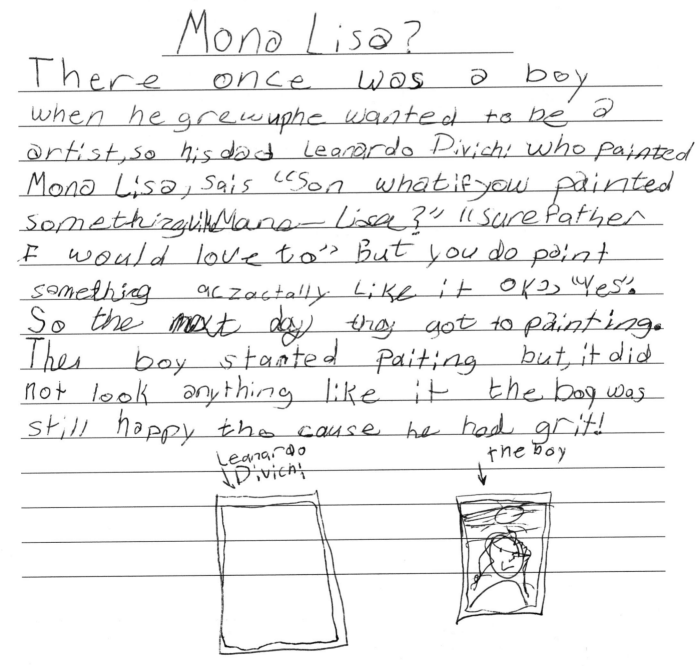

Mona Lisa?

There once was a boy when he grewuphe wanted to be a artist,so hisdad Leanardo Divichi who painted Mona Lisa, sais "Son whatif you painted somethinglikMana Lisa?" "sure Father I would love to" But you do paint something aczactally like it OK,, "Yes". So the next day, they got to painting. The boy started paiting but, it did not look anything like it the boy was still happy tho cause he had grit!

Leanardo Divichi

the boy

Choose a Topic and Organize Ideas

A paragraph should be about one specific topic. After you choose a topic, you then make a list of ideas or details to use when writing about that topic.

In the box is a list of four topics you might choose to write about. Below the box are four idea lists. First write the correct topic above each list of ideas or details. Then, add one idea to each list.

grandparents	television	birthdays	olympics

1. **Topic:** _____

_____

- always ready to buy me a treat
- treat me like a princess

- think I do everything right

_____

2. **Topic:** _____

_____

- like to go to birthday parties
- get to eat ice cream and cake

- play games and win prizes

_____

3. **Topic:** _____

_____

- watch opening ceremony
- skiing races exciting

- also like the bobsled races

_____

4. **Topic:** _____

_____

- especially like shows about nature
- fun to watch Tiger Woods play golf

- like to watch college basketball

_____

Choose a Topic and Organize Ideas *(cont.)*

Paragraph Web

Use this paragraph web to help plan and organize your ideas for a paragraph. Choose a topic from page 10 or any other subject about which you would like to write.

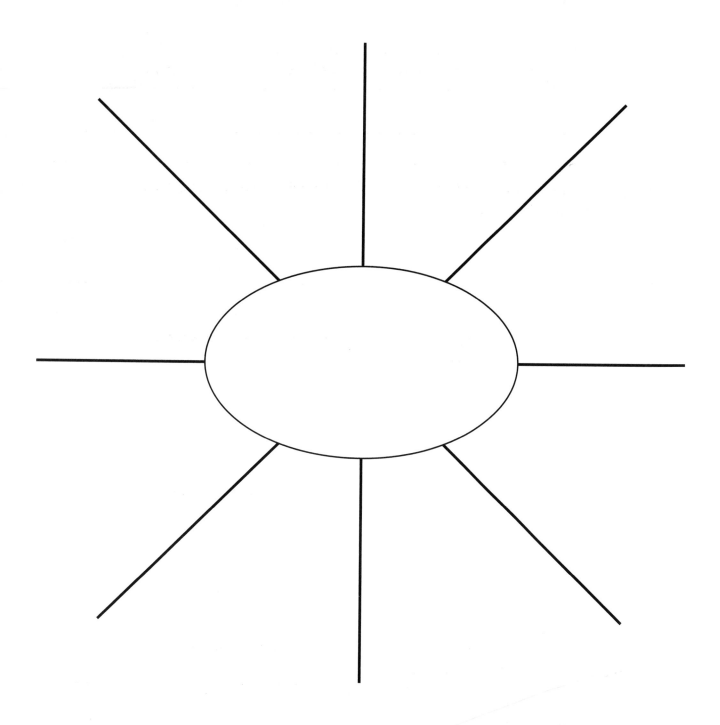

Put Ideas in Order

Once you have selected your topic and have thought of at least three ideas or details about it, you need to decide the order in which to write them. One basic kind of organization is chronological order in which you write events in the order they happened—what happened first, second, and third.

Put these lists of events into chronological order by numbering them from first (1) to last (5).

1. _____ eat breakfast

   _____ get up

   _____ go to school

   _____ go out the door

   _____ brush teeth

2. _____ bait a hook

   _____ clean a fish

   _____ eat a fish

   _____ catch a fish

   _____ cook a fish

3. _____ mail the letter

   _____ put the letter in envelope

   _____ write the letter

   _____ wait for an answer

   _____ seal the letter

4. _____ write a book report

   _____ click on word processing

   _____ turn on printer

   _____ turn on computer

   _____ print book report

5. _____ slap my arm

   _____ see a mosquito

   _____ feel a bite

   _____ hear a buzz

   _____ scratch a bump

6. _____ buy popcorn

   _____ leave the theater

   _____ stand in line

   _____ buy a ticket

   _____ watch a movie

Put Ideas in Order *(cont.)*

Sentences in paragraphs need to be connected. The words used to connect ideas are called *transitions*. These transitions help lead your reader from one idea to the next one.

Using the transition words in parentheses, connect the sentences below and write them in paragraph form.

1. I'll eat a salad.

   I feel like eating a hot, cheesy pizza.

   I've been eating too many pizzas lately.

   (*however, instead, today*)

   Today I feel like eating a hot, cheesy pizza. However, _____

   _____

2. She made me do my homework.

   My mother rushed in and unplugged my CD player.

   I was enjoying music in my room.

   (*suddenly, after that*)

   _____

   _____

   _____

3. I sprinkle everything with nuts.

   I pour fudge or strawberry over the scoops.

   I love to make ice-cream sundaes.

   I scoop ice cream into bowls.

   (*first, then, finally*)

   _____

   _____

   _____

Assessment: Plan a Paragraph

Create a topic sentence based on the details of Rebecca's week. Then put the details in chronological order. Use transition words to create a bridge from sentence to sentence.

Rebecca's Week

_____ 1. Write my book report on Thursday.

_____ 2. Call Janet on Saturday.

_____ 3. Go to baseball practice on Wednesday.

_____ 4. Bake cookies for school on Tuesday.

_____ 5. Prepare my schedule for the week on Monday.

_____ 6. Practice the violin on Friday.

_____

_____

_____

_____

_____

_____

_____

_____

_____

_____

_____

Assessment: Plan a Paragraph *(cont.)*

Chronological Web

Use the web to plan a paragraph for a topic that can be organized in chronological order. You may add more supporting details to the web.

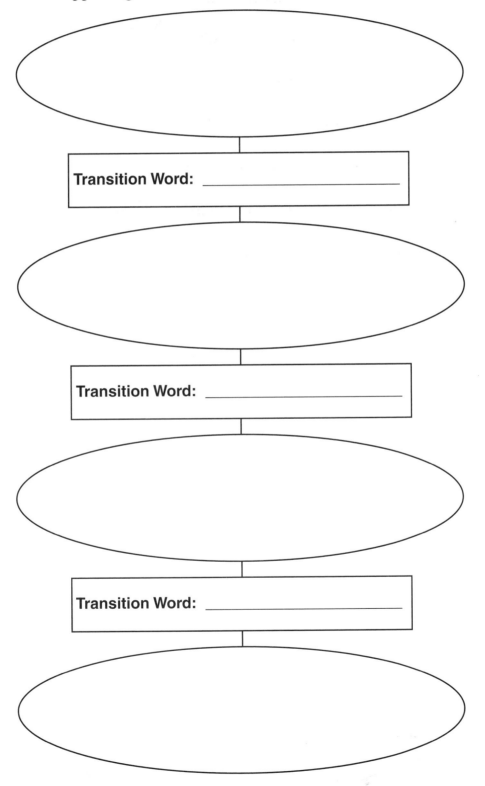

Beginning: Topic Sentence

The topic sentence may be the most important sentence in a paragraph because it tells the reader what the paragraph is about. Underline the topic sentence in this paragraph.

Trees give us many things. They give us shade on hot days. Their wood helps to build our homes. Their leaves give oxygen to the air to help us breathe. They are beautiful to look at, too. What would we do without trees?

Create a topic sentence for each main idea below.

1. dancing

_____

2. a dictionary

_____

3. running shoes

_____

4. a dog

_____

5. bubble gum

_____

6. winter

_____

Beginning: Topic Sentence *(cont.)*

Write a topic sentence for each paragraph below. Remember to indent the first line.

1. _____

_____

_____

      There are lions and tigers in outdoor pens. Wild birds are flying in large, tree-filled cages. Also a visitor at the zoo can see snakes and reptiles of many different sizes. My favorite thing to see at the zoo is the monkey that swings on a trapeze in a cage by the popcorn stand.

◆   ◆   ◆

2. _____

_____

_____

      First, you must listen carefully in class. Next, you must study for your tests and quizzes. Finally, you must do all the homework the teacher assigns. If you follow these steps, good grades will surely be yours.

◆   ◆   ◆

3. _____

_____

_____

      It starts slowly and then destroys everything in its path. It can ruin homes and forests. It can kill people and animals. Before you strike a match, remember how dangerous fire can be.

Middle: Supporting Sentences

Supporting sentences or details expand the topic sentence. They help make the topic or main idea clearer and give more information about it.

There are three topics listed on this page. In the box below, find the three helping or supporting details for each one.

steering wheels	**climbing roses**	**ovens**
refrigerators	**tires**	**daisies**
zinnias	**dishwashers**	**bumpers**

Write a topic sentence for each topic. Develop the details from the Word Bank into supporting sentences.

1. **Topic:** car parts

   Supporting details: _____

   _____

   _____

2. **Topic:** kitchen appliances

   Supporting details: _____

   _____

   _____

3. **Topic:** flower garden

   Supporting details: _____

   _____

   _____

Middle: Supporting Sentences *(cont.)*

Develop the topic sentences by writing at least three supporting sentences for each one.

1. I should receive an "A" on this assignment for three reasons.

_____

_____

_____

_____

2. My mother is one of the most generous people I know.

_____

_____

_____

_____

3. My method for making sandwiches is a very simple one.

_____

_____

_____

_____

End: Concluding Sentence

The final sentence of a paragraph is the closing or concluding sentence. It comes at the end of the supporting details or the body of the paragraph. The conclusion should express the feeling, attitude, or point of the paragraph. Add concluding sentences to the following paragraphs.

1.   My flower garden put on a spectacular show this spring. First, my roses of gold, dark red, and white were heavy with blossoms. Then, the purple pansies at their feet provided a striking, colorful contrast. The space between was filled with the pale yellow, orange, and pink blooms of the poppies I planted.

Concluding sentence:_____

_____

◆   ◆   ◆

2.   My younger brother Jackie can be a big nuisance. His main fault is that he cannot mind his own business and stay out of my room. He snoops around in my closet and desk drawers and leaves my clothes and papers and books in a mess. Whenever we try to work together, he starts a fight. Instead of working in the garden the other day, he sprayed me with the hose.

Concluding sentence:_____

_____

◆   ◆   ◆

3.   Until yesterday, I thought that Juliana was my best friend. That was before I found out that she was telling other people all of the secrets I have told her all year long. I know this is true because Christina came up to me during recess yesterday and told me two of the secrets I had told Juliana. Then, when I talked to Juliana about it, she denied the whole thing.

Concluding sentence: _____

_____

End: Concluding Sentence *(cont.)*

Write concluding sentences for these paragraphs.

1. Our School Band

I enjoy being in our school band. Most people agree that it is a good idea to learn how to play a musical instrument. But there are other good things about our school band, too. It is a place where I can meet many different people and make good friends who share my musical interests. In addition, I get the chance to go to band competitions and march in parades.

_____

_____

_____

◆   ◆   ◆

2. My Favorite Transportation: A Car

When I want to travel, I prefer to go by car. Unlike flying, car travel provides the chance to stop whenever there is an interesting site to explore and to take in the scenery as I drive along. Driving a car is even better than riding on a train because I can get out of the car whenever I want to. If I am on a train, I have to wait until the train pulls into a station before I can get off. Also, I don't have to worry about how others might be inconvenienced by what I want to do.

_____

_____

_____

Assessment: Develop a Paragraph

Choose a topic for a paragraph and write it on the topic lines. Then list three or four supporting details for your topic.

Topic: _____

Supporting details: _____

_____

_____

Compose a topic sentence for your topic. Develop supporting details into sentences for the body of the paragraph.

Topic sentence:_____

_____

Supporting sentences: _____

_____

_____

_____

_____

_____

Assessment: Develop a Paragraph *(cont.)*

Develop a concluding sentence for the paragraph you began on page 22.

Concluding sentence: _____

_____

Create a title for your paragraph. Base it on the content of your topic sentence. Write your paragraph title and your complete paragraph on the lines below.

_____

_____

_____

_____

_____

_____

_____

_____

_____

_____

_____

_____

_____

Add and Remove Details

On the lines below, write the details that do not directly support the topic sentence.

Fishing Is Fun

Fishing is fun for many reasons. It is fun to be out in a boat on a lake or along a stream in the woods. These are places that usually offer peace and quiet as well as an opportunity to catch fish. The most exciting part of fishing is catching a fish, of course. It is also exciting to ride a roller coaster at Disneyland. Until I actually have the fish in the net, I am not sure that I am going to be able to keep him on the hook. Captain Hook was a notorious pirate. If I do manage to catch a fish, I get to enjoy one of the best parts of fishing. That is eating my daily catch that has been cooked over an open fire. You should always be very careful around open fires. It is hard to beat fishing when it comes to having a good time.

_____

_____

_____

_____

_____

_____

_____

_____

Add and Remove Details *(cont.)*

Choose a topic to write a paragraph about and write it on the line below.

Topic: _____

List six supporting details you might use for your topic. Carefully review your list and remove three of the details, leaving the three best supporting details.

_____

_____

_____

_____

_____

_____

Write the remaining three details on the lines below.

_____

_____

_____

Vary Sentence Structure

One way to improve the quality of the sentences in your paragraphs is to combine short, simple sentences into one sentence by using words in a series. You can also form compound sentences by using commas and conjunctions such as *and*, *but*, and *or*. See the examples in the box.

Jarrod is tall. Jarrod is dark. Jarrod is handsome.

Jarrod is **tall**, **dark**, and **handsome**.

Jennylee did not think Josh was handsome. She thought Jarrod was handsome.

Jennylee did not think Josh was handsome, **but** she thought Jarrod was handsome.

Combine these simple sentences into single sentences by using words in a series or by creating compound sentences.

1. Carol and Maria are best friends. They do everything together. They want to be sisters.

   _____

   _____

2. Gavin plays three favorite sports. He plays baseball. He plays basketball. He bowls.

   _____

   _____

3. The children were out of school for the day. They played a game together. They had fun.

   _____

   _____

Vary Sentence Structure *(cont.)*

Kirk and Kristen at the Beach

Kirk and Kristen went to the beach. Kirk and Kristin did many different things there. Kirk and Kristin put on sunscreen as soon as they got out on the sand. Kirk and Kristin decided to build a sandcastle with a moat. Kirk and Kristin next decided to go look for exotic sea creatures in tide pools. Kirk and Kristin decided it was time to eat lunch. Kirk and Kristen rested for awhile after lunch. Kirk and Kristin went into the water. Kirk and Kristin played volleyball. Kirk and Kristin went home after an enjoyable day at the beach.

_____

_____

_____

_____

_____

_____

_____

_____

_____

_____

_____

_____

_____

Improve Word Choice

Nouns: Substitute exact or more specific nouns for the vague nouns in italics.

   Example: That *thing* was horrid. That *spider* was horrid.

1. Dad worked at his desk for a *time*.

2. The *book* was enjoyable.

3. We visited that historic *place*.

4. My brother put *pieces* together.

5. I added *stuff* to the recipe.

Verbs: Substitute exact or more vivid verbs for the vague verbs in italics.

   Example: Max *walked* home. Max *marched* home.

1. I *ran* to catch the early bus.

2. Lori *likes* pizza with extra cheese.

3. That pitcher *throws* a wicked fast ball.

4. Our teacher *said* the directions three times.

5. Big Hank *ate* five potato pancakes.

Improve Word Choice *(cont.)*

Adjectives: In addition to using the noun substitutes you made on the previous page, add exact adjectives to describe them.

    Example: That *gigantic spider* was horrid.

  1. Dad worked at his desk for a *time.*

    _____

  2. The *story* was enjoyable.

    _____

  3. We visited that historic *place.*

    _____

  4. My brother put *pieces* together.

    _____

  5. I added *stuff* to the recipe.

    _____

Adverbs: In addition to using the verb substitutes you made on the previous page, add exact adverbs to describe them.

    Example: Max *merrily marched* home.

  1. I *ran* to catch the early bus.

    _____

  2. Lori *likes* pizza with extra cheese.

    _____

  3. That pitcher *throws* a wicked fast ball.

    _____

  4. Our teacher *said* the directions three times.

    _____

  5. Big Hank *ate* five potato pancakes.

    _____

Use Imagery: Similes

A **simile** is a direct comparison between two unrelated things. A simile shows how the two things are alike in one special way. The words *like* or *as* are used to make the comparison.

Example: Oliver swims *like* a fish.

The phrases below are the beginnings of similes. Complete each one, making a sentence. You may add more than one word.

1. Our lazy cat sleeps like _____

2. The hospital emergency room was as busy as _____

3. Autumn leaves are falling just like _____

4. On my birthday, I am as happy as _____

5. The leftover meatloaf tasted like _____

6. After work, Mother is as hungry as a _____

Create similes of your own to describe the following:

1. the color of the sunset _____

2. the feeling you have on the first day of school _____

3. a butterfly on its way south _____

4. the way a newborn puppy feels in your hands _____

Use Imagery: Metaphors

A **metaphor** is an indirect comparison between two unrelated things. A metaphor describes a likeness that exists in one special way. The words *like* or *as* are *not* used in a metaphor. A metaphor states one thing acts like or appears to be another.

Example: Justin *is a pig* at the table. (metaphor)

Justin eats *like a pig*. (simile)

The following phrases are the beginnings of metaphors. Complete each one, making a sentence. You may add more than one word.

1. The moon is _____

2. The stale crackers were _____

3. A scientist's mind is _____

4. The dirty fishbowl is _____

5. A flexible gymnast is _____

6. The cries of the tiny baby were _____

Create metaphors of your own to describe the following:

1. your bedroom _____

2. a nearby park _____

3. a baby bird _____

4. a new house _____

Assessment: Revise and Edit a Paragraph

To revise and edit the paragraph, do the following:

- Put the topic sentence, supporting details, and conclusion in order.
- Use transition words.
- Add and remove details as needed.

- Vary sentence structure.
- Improve word choice.
- Use imagery.

Work on revising the paragraph on this page and then write your final copy on the next page.

My Older Sister

She was in my room again yesterday. She thinks she always has to check on me even if there is an adult in the house. She doesn't just look around. She gets into my things. She had been eating pizza. She even asks me questions about my friends. One of her best friends is a gossip. She also asks me how I am doing in school. She asks me about my grades. She wants to know if I get along with my teacher. She probably thinks I should ask her permission before I go anywhere or do anything. She is the most annoying older sister you could ever imagine. She should not try to run my life.

Assessment: Revise and Edit a Paragraph *(cont.)*

Write your final copy of "My Older Sister." You may give the sister a name. You also may change the title of the paragraph to better fit the topic sentence.

_____

Check Grammar, Capitalization, Punctuation, Spelling

After you have proofread your "My Older Sister" paragraph and have corrected all the grammar, capitalization, punctuation, and spelling, write the proofread copy below and compare it with the copy on the preceding page.

_____

_____

_____

_____

_____

_____

_____

_____

_____

_____

Paragraph Checklist

Use this checklist as part of the process whenever you write a paragraph. You should use it as a guide when you write your paragraphs for Section 6.

- Prewriting, planning, organizing
- One main idea or topic
- List of supporting details in order
- Topic sentence developed
- Supporting details added
- Supporting details sentences developed
- Concluding sentence developed
- Nonessential details removed
- Varied sentence structures
- Transitions used
- Word choice improved (nouns, verbs, adjectives, adverbs)
- Similes and metaphors used
- Grammar checked
- Capitalization checked
- Punctuation checked
- Spelling checked

Descriptions of Paragraphs and Sample Topics

Expository Paragraph

Expository writing gives facts, explains ideas, or gives directions. It is nonfiction writing that informs your reader or that explains how to do something. The following are some sample expository paragraph topics: how to ride a bike, how to write a poem, why you like your favorite sport (or any other pastime), or how a camera works.

◆ ◆ ◆

Narrative Paragraph

A narrative paragraph gives the details of an experience or event in story form. It usually explains what happened in chronological order. Usually the most interesting narrative writing occurs when the writer relates an unusual or exciting true experience. However, narrative writing may also be fictional. The following are some sample narrative paragraph topics: the first time you ever did something, a time you were embarrassed, the last day of something (kindergarten, vacation), a visit, a trip, etc.

◆ ◆ ◆

Autobiographical Paragraph

Both expository and narrative paragraphs may be autobiographical, but that is not a requirement. An autobiographical paragraph must relate an episode from your own life. The topics listed for the narrative paragraph are also examples of those used for the autobiographical paragraph.

◆ ◆ ◆

Friendly Letter

The form of a friendly letter is less formal than that of a business letter. Its heading consists of three lines: two for the writer's address and one for the date. A comma follows both the greeting and the closing. The body is usually two or three paragraphs.

Friendly Letter and Envelope Forms

heading

(address line 1) _____

(address line 2) _____

date _____

greeting

Dear _____,

(body, one or more paragraphs) _____

_____

_____

_____

_____

closing

Sincerely yours,

_____

(signature)

---

writer's name, line 1 _____

address, line 2 _____

address, line 3

stamp

recipient's name, line 1
recipient's address, line 2
recipient's address, line 3

Write an Expository Paragraph

Make a plan for writing a paragraph to explain how to do something or give facts or directions. Plan your paragraph:

- Choose a topic.
- Develop a topic sentence.
- Make a list of supporting details to develop into body sentences.
- Compose a concluding sentence.

Topic sentence

_____

_____

List of details

_____

_____

_____

_____

_____

Concluding sentence

_____

_____

Write an Expository Paragraph *(cont.)*

Write the title of your paragraph on the first line and then use your paragraph plan to write your expository paragraph.

_____

_____

_____

_____

_____

_____

_____

_____

_____

_____

_____

_____

Write a Narrative Paragraph

Make a plan for writing about an experience or an event. Plan your paragraph:

- Choose a topic.
- Develop a topic sentence.
- Make a list of supporting details to develop into body sentences.
- Compose a concluding sentence.

Topic sentence

_____

_____

List of details

_____

_____

_____

_____

_____

Concluding sentence

_____

_____

Write a Narrative Paragraph *(cont.)*

Write the title of your paragraph on the first line and then use your paragraph plan to write your narrative paragraph.

_____

_____

_____

_____

_____

_____

_____

_____

_____

_____

_____

Write an Autobiographical Paragraph

Make a plan for writing about an episode from your life. Plan your paragraph:

- Choose a topic.
- Develop a topic sentence.
- Make a list of supporting details to develop into body sentences.
- Compose a concluding sentence.

Topic sentence

_____

_____

List of details

_____

_____

_____

_____

_____

Concluding sentence

_____

_____

Write an Autobiographical
Paragraph *(cont.)*

Write the title of your paragraph on the first line and then use your paragraph plan to write your autobiographical paragraph.

_____

_____

_____

_____

_____

_____

_____

_____

_____

_____

_____

_____

Write a Friendly Letter

Make a plan for writing a letter to a friend. Your friend may live nearby or far away. Plan your friendly letter:

- Respond to letters you have received in the past.
- Tell about your most recent activities.
- Report any special news.
- Refer to any mutual friends and/or your family.

Response to previous correspondence

_____

_____

Most recent activities

_____

_____

Special news

_____

_____

Mutual friends, family

_____

_____

Write a Friendly Letter *(cont.)*

Write a letter to a friend and address an envelope to send it in. Don't forget to put on a stamp before you mail it. Use the form on this page to compose your letter.

_____

_____

_____

_____

_____

_____

_____

_____

_____

_____

_____

_____

_____

_____

Unit Assessment

Read the paragraph and answer the questions that follow it. Fill in the circles beside the correct answers.

Happy on Rainy Days

(1) Rainy days do not make me blue because I can always find productive, enjoyable, and relaxing activities which help me pass the time happily on rainy days. (2) Usually, the first thing I do is write letters to my friends and relatives. (3) My grandparents seem to appreciate hearing from me more than anyone, so I always write to them first. (4) Next, I turn my attention to the kitchen where I bake brownies from my secret brownie recipe. My neighbor Martha calls them chocolate dreams. (5) Mine are the most delicious brownies in the entire neighborhood. (6) By the time I have finished writing and baking, I am ready for some relaxation. (7) For that, I turn to reading. (8) When I become lost in a good book, the hours pass quickly. (9) Because I enjoy writing, baking, and reading, rainy days are happy days.

1. Which is the topic sentence?
   - a. (1)
   - b. (2)
   - c. (7)
   - d. (8)
   - e. (9)

2. How many body sentences are there?
   - a. 5
   - b. 7
   - c. 9
   - d. 3
   - e. 2

3. Which is the concluding sentence?
   - a. (5)
   - b. (6)
   - c. (9)
   - d. (8) and (9)
   - e. none of these

4. Which three supporting details did the writer most likely have on her list?
   - a. grandparents, kitchen, book
   - b. friends, grandparents, brownies
   - c. reading, baking, writing letters
   - d. relaxation, reading, rain
   - e. mail, dreams, hours

5. In addition to the word "rain," what other word is used throughout the paragraph to support the main idea?
   - a. enjoyable
   - b. happy
   - c. writing
   - d. reading
   - e. relaxing

6. Which of the following words is used as a transition word?
   - a. By
   - b. Martha
   - c. Next
   - d. My
   - e. Mine

Unit Assessment (cont.)

7. Which expression is a metaphor?

   ○ a. "make me blue"

   ○ b. "always write to them first"

   ○ c. "in the entire neighborhood"

   ○ d. "help me pass the time happily"

   ○ e. "one of my friends"

8. Which kind of paragraph is this?

   ○ a. narrative

   ○ b. expository

   ○ c. friendly letter

   ○ d. comparison

   ○ e. none of these

9. Which of these words is used as an adjective to describe the noun "recipe"?

   ○ a. delicious

   ○ b. secret

   ○ c. rainy

   ○ d. enjoyable

   ○ e. entire

10. Which of these words is used as an adverb to describe the verb "pass"?

    ○ a. some

    ○ b. ready

    ○ c. always

    ○ d. happily

    ○ e. lost

11. Which word is the only proper noun used in the paragraph?

    ○ a. grandparents

    ○ b. book

    ○ c. Martha

    ○ d. brownies

    ○ e. dreams

12. Which sentence contains a series of words separated by commas?

    ○ a. (6)

    ○ b. (3)

    ○ c. (1)

    ○ d. (8)

    ○ e. (9)

13. Which of these groups of sentences could be removed from the paragraph without hurting the basic structure and content?

    ○ a. (1, 3, 4)

    ○ b. (7, 8, 9)

    ○ c. (5, 8, 9)

    ○ d. (2, 5, 9)

    ○ e. none of these

14. Which of these titles could also be used for this paragraph?

    ○ a. Rainy Days Are Cute

    ○ b. Rainy Day Make Me Sad

    ○ c. I Hate Rainy Days

    ○ d. No Rainy Days for Me

    ○ e. Love Those Rainy Days

Answer Key

page 4

1. IT
2. D
3. E
4. IP
5. IT
6. D
7. IP
8. D
9. E
10 D

page 5

1. When, Mrs. Lee
2. My, Disneyland, July
3. On Wednesday, Groundhog Day
4. In, August, Aunt Mary, San Francisco, California
5. My, Julia, Paris, France, June
6. I, *Old Yeller*
7. My, Rosa, Spanish, I, English
8. Benjie, Happy Birthday, You

page 6

It was a clear, calm day on April 1, 2002, when I was a student at Oak Grove Elementary School in Oak Grove, Montana. My teacher came into the classroom and smiled. Suddenly, Jeffrey jumped up and said, 'Oh!" said Glenda, "Where is the spider?" "Mrs. Lee, there's a spider crawling on your head." Mrs. Lee pretended that she was afraid, but only for a minute. Then Jeffrey yelled, "April Fool!" We all laughed. Then Mrs. Lee explained how the first day of April is always April Fools' Day.

page 7

One day a boy woke up to get ready for school. He washed his face and combed his hair. Then he put on the red shirt and blue jeans that his mother had laid out for him. It took some time to put on his shoes because the laces were tied in double knots. Finally, he did it. Afterwards, he went to the kitchen to eat some cereal and milk. It was very good. Then he remembered he needed to pack a lunch. He made a peanut butter and jelly sandwich, and he put it in his lunchbox with an apple and some cookies. Now he was ready. But wait! He forgot to brush his teeth. He brushed them quickly and finished just as the bus was pulling up. Then the boy was off to school.

page 9

A Night at the Circus

I love to go to the circus. On May 6, 2002, the circus came to my hometown of Jackson, Wyoming. A parade marched through our streets, and soon the big top could be seen. Ken and I went to watch the performers prepare for opening night. We saw clowns, acrobats, and even the ringmaster. What a sight! Have you ever seen anything like it? You should go if you ever get the chance to spend a night at the circus.

page 10

1. Grandparents
2. Birthdays
3. Olympics
4. Television

page 12

(Accept logical variations.)

1. 2, 1, 5, 4, 3
2. 1, 3, 5, 2, 4
3. 4, 2, 1, 5, 3
4. 4, 2, 3, 1, 5
5. 4, 3, 2, 1, 5
6. 3, 5, 1, 2, 4

page 14

4, 6, 3, 2, 1, 5

page 24

It is always exciting to ride a roller coaster at Disneyland.

Captain Hook was a notorious pirate.

You should always be very careful around open fires.

pages 46 and 47

1. a	8. b
2. b	9. b
3. c	10. d
4. c	11. c
5. b	12. e
6. c	13. e
7. a	14. e